AN INTRODUCTION TO THE STUDY OF THE KABALAH

WILLIAM WYNN WESTCOTT

SCRIBERE SEMPER ET LEGERE

CONTENTS

PREFACE

Students of literature, philosophy and religion who have any sympathy with the Occult Sciences may well pay some attention to the Kabalah of the Hebrew Rabbis of olden times; for whatever faith may be held by the enquirer he will gain not only knowledge, but also will broaden his views of life and destiny, by comparing other forms of religion with the faith and doctrines in which he has been nurtured, or which he has adopted after reaching full age and powers of discretion.

Being fully persuaded of the good to be thus derived, I desire to call attention to the dogmas of the old Hebrew Kabalah. I had the good fortune to be attracted to this somewhat recondite study, at an early period of life, and I have been able to spare a little time in subsequent years to collect some knowledge of this Hebrew religious philosophy; my information upon the subject has been enlarged by my membership of The Rosicrucian Society.

Yet the Kabalistic books are so numerous and so lengthy, and so many of them only to be studied in Rabbinic Hebrew and Chaldee that I feel to-day less confident of my knowledge of the Kabalah than I did twenty years ago, when this essay was first published, after delivery in the form of lectures to a Society of Hermetic Students in 1888.

Since that date a French translation of "The Zohar," by Jean de Pauly, and a work entitled "The Literature and History of the Kabalah," by Arthur E. Waite, have been published, yet I think that this little treatise will be found of interest to those who have not sufficient leisure to master the more complete works on the Kabalah.

The Old Testament has been of necessity referred to, but I have by intention made no references to the New Testament, or to the faith and doctrines taught by Jesus the Christ, as the Saviour of the

world: if any desire to refer to the alleged refer-
ence in the Kabalah to the Trinity, it will be found
in the Zohar ii., 43, b.: and an English version of
the same in "The Kabbalah," by C. D. Ginsburg.

WM. WYNN WESTCOTT, M.B., etc.

THE KABALAH

It must be confessed that the origin of the Kabalah is lost in the mists of antiquity; no one can demonstrate who was its author, or who were its earliest teachers.

Considerable evidence may be adduced to show that its roots pass back to the Hebrew Rabbis who flourished at the time of the Second Temple about the year 515 B.C. Of its existence before that time I know of no proofs.

It has been suggested that the captivity of the Jews in Babylon led to the formation of this philosophy by the effect of Chaldean lore and dogma acting on Jewish tradition. No doubt in the earliest stages of its existence the teaching was entirely oral, hence the name QBLH from QBL to receive, and it became varied by the minds through which it filtered in its course; there is no proof that any part of it was written for centuries after. It has been kept curiously distinct both from the Exoteric Pentateuchal Mosaic books, and from the ever-growing Commentaries upon them, the Mishna and Gemara, which form the Talmud. This seems to have grown up in Hebrew theology without combining with the recondite doctrines of the Kabalah. In a similar manner we see in India that the Upanishads, an Esoteric series of treatises, grew up alongside the Brahmanas and the Puranas, which are Exoteric instructions designed for the use of the masses of the people.

With regard to the oldest Kabalistic books still extant, a controversy has raged among modern critics, who deny the asserted era of each work, and try to show that the assumed author is the only person who could not have written each one in question. But these critics show the utmost divergence of opinion the moment it becomes necessary to fix on a date or an author; so much more easy is destructive criticism than the acquirement of real knowledge.

Let us make a short note of the chief of the old Kabalistic treatises.

The "Sepher Yetzirah" or "Book of Formation" is the oldest treatise; it is attributed by legend to Abraham the Patriarch: several editions of an English translation by myself have been published. This work explains a most curious philosophical scheme of Creation, drawing a parallel between the origin of the world, the sun, the planets, the elements, seasons, man and the twenty-two letters of the Hebrew alphabet; dividing them into a Triad, a Heptad and a Dodecad; three mother letters A, M, and Sh are referred to primeval Air, Water and Fire; seven double letters are referred to the planets and the sevenfold division of time, etc.: and the twelve simple letters are referred to the months, zodiacal signs and human organs. Modern criticism tends to the conclusion that the existing ancient versions were compiled about A.D. 200. The "Sepher Yetzirah" is mentioned in the Talmuds, both of Jerusalem and of Babylon; it was written in the Neo-Hebraic language, like the Mishna.

The "Zohar" or" Sohar" spelled in Hebrew ZHR or ZUHR "The Book of Splendour" or of "Light," is a collection of many separate treatises on the Deity,

Angels, Souls and Cosmogony. Its authorship is ascribed to Rabbi Simon ben Jochai, who lived A.D. 160; he was persecuted and driven to live in a cave by Lucius Aurelius Verus, co-regent with the Emperor Marcus Aurelius Antoninus. Some considerable portion of the work may have been arranged by him from the oral traditions of his time: but other parts have certainly been added by other hands at intervals up to the time when it was first published as a whole by Rabbi Moses de Leon, of Guadalajara in Spain, circa 1290. From that time its history is known; printed Editions have been issued in Mantua, 1558, Cremona, 1560, and Lublin, 1623; these are the three famous Codices of "The Zohar" in the Hebrew language. For those who do not read Hebrew the only practical means of studying the Zohar are the partial translation into Latin of Baron Knorr von Rosenroth, published in 1684 under the title of "Kabbala Denudata"; and the English edition of three treatises,--"Siphra Dtzenioutha" or "Book of Concealed Mystery"; "Ha Idra Rabba," "Greater Assembly"; and "Ha Idra Suta," " Lesser Assembly," translated by S. L. MacGregor Mathers. These three books give a fair idea of the tone, style and material of the Zohar but they only include a partial view: other tracts in the Zohar are :--

Hikaloth--The Palaces, Sithre Torah--Mysteries of the Law, Midrash ha Neelam--The secret commentary, Raja Mehemna—The faithful shepherd, Saba Demishpatim,--The discourse of the Aged-- the prophet Elias, and Januka-- The Young man; with Notes called Tosephta and Mathanithan.

In course of publication there is now a French translation of the complete Zohar, by Jean de Pauly: this is a most scholarly work.

Other famous Kabalistic treatises are :-- "The Commentary on the Ten Sephiroth," by Rabbi Azariel ben Menachem, 1200 A.D. ; "The Alphabet" of Rabbi Akiba; " The Gate of Heaven" ; the "Book of Enoch"; "Pardes Rimmonim, or Garden of Pomegrantes"; "A treatise on the Emanations"; "Otz ha Chiim, or The Tree of Life" of Chajim Vital; "Rashith ha Galgulim, or Revolutions of Souls" of Isaac de Loria; and especially the writings of the famous Spanish Jew, Ibn Gebirol, who died A.D. 1070, and was also called Avicebron, his great works are "The fountain of life" and "The Crown of the Kingdom."

The teaching of the Kabalah has been considered to be grouped into several schools, each of which was for a time famous. I may mention :--The

School of Gerona, 1190 to 1210, of Rabbi Isaac the Blind, Rabbis Azariel and Ezra, and Moses Nachmanides. The School of Segovia of Rabbis Jacob, Abulafia (died 1305), Shem Tob (died 1332), and Isaac of Akko. The School of Rabbi Isaac ben Abraham Ibn Latif about 1390. The School of Abulafia (died 1292) and Joseph Gikatilla (died 1300); also the Schools of "Zoharists" of Rabbis Moses de Leon (died 1305), Menahem di Recanti (died 1350), Isaac Loria (died 1572) and Chajim Vital, who died in 1620. A very famous German Kabalist was John Reuchlin or Capnio, and he wrote two great works, the "De Verbo Mirifico," and "De arte Cabalistica."

In the main there were two tendencies among the Kabalists: the one set devoted themselves entirely to the doctrinal and dogmatic branch: the other to the practical and wonder-working aspect.

The greatest of the wonder-working Rabbis were Isaac Loria, also called Ari; and Sabatai Zevi, who curiously enough became a Mahommedan. Both of these departments of Occult Rabbinic lore have their living representatives, chiefly scattered individuals; very rarely groups of initiates are found. In Central Europe, parts of Russia, Austria and

Poland there are even now Jews, known as Wonderworking Rabbis, who can do strange things they attribute to the Kabalah, and things very difficult to explain have been seen in England, at the hands of students of Kabalistic rites and talismans.

The Rabbinic Commentaries, many series deep, overlaying each other, which now exist in connection with the old treatises form such a mass of Kabalistic lore as to make it an almost impossible task to grasp them; probably no Christian nor Jew in this country can say what doctrines are not still laid up in some of the old manuscript works.

The Dogmatic or Theoretical Kabalah indicates philosophical conceptions respecting the Deity, Angels and beings more spiritual than man; the human Soul and its several aspects or parts; concerning pre-existence and re-incarnation and the several worlds or planes of existence.

The Practical Kabalah attempts a mystical and allegorical interpretation of the Old Testament, studying each phrase, word and letter; it teaches the connection between letters and numbers and the modes of their inter-relation; the principles of Gematria, Notaricon, and Temura; the formation and uses of the divine and angelic names as

Amulets; the formation of Magic Squares; and a vast fund of allied curious lore, which subsequently formed the basis of Mediaeval Magic.

For those who do not wish to read any Kabalistic work as a whole, but rather to glean a general view of this philosophy, there are now three standard works; two are in English; one by Dr. C. Ginsburg, 1865, a formal and concise resume of the doctrines; the other, an excellent book, "The Doctrine and Literature of the Kabalah," by Arthur E. Waite, 1902; and one in French by Adolph Franck, 1889, which is more discursive and gives fewer details.

Many points of the teaching of Indian systems of religious philosophy are not touched on by the Hebrew system, or are excluded by differences of a fundamental nature: such as the Cosmogony of other Worlds, unless the destroyed Worlds of Unbalanced Force refer to these; the inviolability of law, as Karma, is not a prominent feature; Reincarnation is taught, but the number of re-births is limited generally to three.

Some small part of the Kabalistic doctrine is found in the Jewish Talmud, but in that collection of treatises there is some grossness that is absent from the true Kabalah; such are the theories of the debasement of men into animal forms; and of men to be re-born as women, as a punishment for earthly sins in a previous life.

It must be remembered that many points of doctrine are limited to the teachings of but a few Rabbis; and that the differences between the earliest and latest doctrines on a given point are sometimes very great, as is shown by a comparison of the Books of the Rabbis of different eras and schools. Some of the Kabalistic teaching has also never been printed nor published, and has been handed down even to this day from master to pupil only: there are some points not found in any Hebrew book, which I myself have taught in the Rosicrucian Society and in Hermetic Lodges. An attentive study of some of these old mystical Hebrew books discloses the existence of intentional "blinds," which appear to have been introduced to confine certain dogmas to certain students fitted to receive them, and to preserve them from promiscuous distribution and so from misuse by the ignorant or vicious.

Two or three centuries have now passed since any notable addition to the body of Kabalistic doctrine has been made, but before that time a long succession of commentaries had been produced, all tending to illustrate or extend the philosophical scheme.

As already said, when the Kabalah first took shape as a concrete whole and a philosophic system, may remain for ever an unknown datum, but if we regard it, as I believe is correct, as the Esotericism of the religion of the Hebrews, the foundation dogmas are doubtless almost as old as the first promulgation of the main principles of the worship of Jehovah.

I cannot now attempt any glance at the contentions of some doubting scholars, who question whether the story of the Twelve Tribes is a historic fact, or whether there ever were a Moses, or even a King Solomon. It is sufficient for the present purpose that the Jewish nation had the Jehovistic theology and a system of priestly caste, and a coherent doctrine, at the time of the Second Temple when Cyrus, Sovereign of all Asia, 536 B.C., holding the Jews in captivity, permitted certain of them to return to Jerusalem for the express purpose of reestablishing the Hebrew mode of worship which had been forcibly interfered with by Nebuchadnezzar in 587 B.C.

After this return to Jerusalem it was that Ezra and Nehemiah, circa 450 B.C., edited and compiled the Old Testament of the Hebrews, or according to those who deny the Mosaic authorship and the Solomonic regime, it was then that they wrote the Pentateuch.

The renewed worship maintained until 320 B.C., when Jerusalem was captured by Ptolemy Soter, who, however, did not destroy the foundations of the Jewish religion; indeed his successor, Ptolemy Philadelphus, caused the Hebrew scriptures to be revised and translated into Greek by Seventy-two scholars, about 277 B.C.; this has been known for centuries as the Septuagint version of the Old Testament.

Further Jewish troubles followed, however, and Jerusalem was again taken and pillaged by Antiochus in 170 B.C. Then followed the long wars of the Maccabees; subsequently the Romans dominated Judea, then quarrelling with the Jews the city was taken by Pompey, and not long after was again plundered by the Roman general Crassus in 54 B.C. Yet the Jewish religion was preserved, and we find the religious feasts and festivals all in progress at the time of Jesus; yet once more in A.D. 70, was the Holy City taken, plundered and burnt, and that by Titus, who became Emperor of the Romans in A.D. 79.

Through all these vicissitudes, the Hebrew Old Testament survived, yet must almost unavoidably have had many alterations and additions made to its several treatises; the more Esoteric doctrines which were handed down along the line of the priestly caste, and not incorporated with the Torah offered to the people, may no doubt have been repeatedly varied by the influences of contending teachers.

Soon after this period was framed the first series of glosses and commentaries on the Old Testament books, which have come down to our times. Of these the earliest are the volume called the "Targum of Onkelos" on "The Law," written about A.D. 100, and that of Jonathan ben Uzziel on "The Prophets."

About A.D 141 there first came into note the now famous treatise written by the Rabbis of Judah, called "Mishna," and this formed the basis of those vast compilations of Hebrew doctrine called the "Talmud," of which there are two extant forms, one compiled at Babylon-the most notable, and the other associated with Jerusalem. To the original "Mishna" the Rabbis added further commentaries named "Gemara." From this time the literature of Judaism grew apace, and there was a constant succession of notable Hebrew Rabbis who published religious treatises, until at least A.D. 1500. The two Talmuds were first printed at Venice in 1520 and 1523 respectively.

The Old Testament books were the guiding light through the ages of the Jews, but the learned Rabbis were not satisfied with them alone, and they supplemented them by two parallel series of works of literature; the one, Talmudic, being commentaries based upon Thirteen Rules of Argument delivered by Moses to illustrate the Old Testament, and supply material for teaching the populace; and the other a long series of treatises of a more abstruse character, designed to illustrate their Secret Doctrines and Esoteric views. The Sepher Yetzirah, and the Zohar or Book of Splendour represent the kernel of that oral instruction which the Rabbis of the olden times prided themselves upon possessing, and which they have even claimed as being "The Secret Knowledge" which God gave to Moses for the use of the priests themselves, in contradistinction to the Written Law intended for the masses of the people.

One of the principal conceptions of the Kabalah is that spiritual wisdom is attained by Thirty-two Paths, typified by the Ten numbers and the Twenty-two letters; these Ten again being symbols of the Divine Emanations, the Sephiroth, the Holy Voices chanting at the Crystal Sea, the Great Sea, the Mother Supernal, Binah; and of the Twenty-two occult forces of the Nature of the Universe symbolised by the Three primary Elements, the Seven Planets, and the Twelve Zodiacal influences of the heavens, which tincture human concerns through the path of our Sun in its annual course. I have given the names and definitions of the Thirty-two Paths at the end of my Edition of the" Sepher Yetzirah."

Now to show the close connection between the Kabalah and orthodox Judaism, we find the Rabbis cataloguing the Books of the Old Testament into a series of Twenty-two (the letters) works to be read for the culture of spiritual life; this Twenty-two they obtained from the Thirty-nine books of the O.T. Canon, by collecting the twelve minor prophets into one treatise; Ruth they added to Judges; Ezra to Nehemiah; while the two books each of Samuel, Kings, and Chronicles, they called one each. The Canon of Thirty-nine works was fixed in the time of Ezra.

Returning to the books which illustrate the Kabalah, whatever may be the authenticity of their alleged origins, it cannot be denied that those ancient volumes, Sepher Yetzirah and Zohar, contain a system of spiritual philosophy of clear design, deep intuition and far-reaching cosmologic suggestions; that are well worthy of the honour of receiving a special name and of founding a theological body of doctrine,--The Kabalah.

The bulwark and main foundation of the public Hebrew religion has always been the Pentateuch, five treatises attributed to Moses, which proclaim the Laws of Jehovah given to his chosen people. The Old Testament beginning with these five books is further continued by historic books, by poetical teachings and by prophetic works, but many portions are marked by materialistic characteristics and a lack of spiritual rectitude which the books of a Great Religion might be expected to display, and they even offend our present standard of moral life.

The Mosaic Law, eminently valuable for many purposes to a small nation 3,000 years ago, and containing many regulations of a type showing great attention to sanitary matters, is yet marred by the application of penalties of gross cruelty and harsh treatment of erring mortals, which are hardly compatible with our modern views of what might have emanated from God the personal Creator of this Universe with its million worlds; and the almost entire absence of any reference to a life after death for human beings shows a materialism which needed a new Revelation by Jesus, whose life has earned the title of "Christ." Yet the orthodox of England hear this statement with incredulity, and if asked to show the passages in the Old Testament which insist on a life after death, or on a succession of lives for purposes of retribution, or the passages demonstrating the immortality of the soul, they could not produce them, and are content to refer you to the clergy, whose answer generally is, "If not plainly laid down, these dogmas are implied." But are they? If they are, how is it that notably clear passages can be quoted which show that important authors in the Old Testament make statements in direct opposition to these doctrines? And how is it, again, that a great author of modern times has said, "Prosperity was the blessing of the Old Testament for good works, but adversity that of the New"? This could only be true if there were no future life or lives, or no coming period of reward and punishment contemplated by the Old Testament doctrine.

But the comment is true and the Old Testament does teach that man is no more immortal than the beast, as witness Ecclesiastes, iii. 19 :--"For that which befalleth the sons of men, befalleth beasts; even one thing befalleth them: as the one dieth, so dieth the other; yea they have all one breath; so that man hath no pre-eminence above a beast: for all is vanity. All go unto one place; all are of the dust, and all turn to dust again. . . . Wherefore I perceive that there is nothing better, than that a man should rejoice in his own works; for that is his portion: for who shall bring him to see what shall be after him?" Who, indeed, except his own Ego, Soul or Higher Self.

But perhaps this book is from the pen of some obscure Jew, or half pagan Chaldee or Babylonian. Not at all: Jewish critics have all assigned it to Solomon, who was the King of the Jews at the time of their heyday of glory; surely if the immortality of the soul were the essence of the Judaism of the people, Solomon could not have so grossly denied it.

Go back, however, to the narrative of Creation in Genesis, and the same story is found; the animals are made from the dust, man is made from the dust, and Eve is made from Adam, and each has breathed into the form, the "Nephesh Chiah,"--the breath of life, vitality; but there is no hint that Adam received a Ray of the Supernal Mind, which was to dwell there for a time, to gain experience, to receive retribution, and then enter another stage of progress, and achieve a final return to its Divine source. And yet the authors of these volumes, whoever they were, could hardly have been without the conception of the higher part of man, of his Spiritual Soul. The critical contention is that the Old Testament was deprived at some period of its religious philosophy, which was set apart for a privileged class; while the husk of strict law and tradition was alone offered for the acceptance of the people. The kernel of spiritual philosophy which is lacking in the Old Testament as a religious book may be the essential core of the Kabalah; for these Kabalistic dogmas are Hebraic, and they are spiritual, and they are sublime in their grandeur; and the Old Testament read by their light becomes a volume worthy of thc acceptance of a nation. I speak of the essentials of the Kabalah, the ancient substratum of the Kabalah. I grant that in many extant treatises these primal truths have been obscured by generations of editors, by visionary and often crude additions, and by the vagaries of Oriental imagery; but the keynotes of a great spiritual Divine concealed Power, of its Emanations in manifestation, of its energising of human life, of the prolonged existence of human souls, and of the temporary state of corporeal existence, are fundamental doctrines there fully illustrated; and these are the points of contact between the Kabalah of the Jew and the so-called Esotericism of the teachings of Buddha and of Hinduism.

It may be that the Catholic Church, from which the Protestant Church seceded, was from its origin in the possession of the Hebrew Rabbinic secret of the intentional Exoteric nature of the Bible, and of a priestly mode of understanding the Esoteric Kabalah, as a key to the true explanations of the Jewish books, which being apparently histories are really largely allegorical. If this were granted, it would explain why the Catholic Church has for ages discouraged the laity from the study of the Old Testament books, and would lead us to think that Protestantism made a mistake in combining with the Reformation of a vicious priesthood the encouragement of the laity to read the Old Testament books.

I note that the literal interpretation of the Mosaic books and those of the Old Testament generally has repeatedly been used as a support for vicious Systems of conduct; a notable example of which was seen even a hundred years ago, when the clergy of Protestant nations almost unanimously supported the continuance of the Slave Trade from arguments derived from the laws of Jehovah as stated to have been compulsory upon the Jews.

The Freethinkers of that day were largely the champions of suffering and oppressed races, and for centuries the wisest of men, the greatest scientists have maintained, and ever won, struggle after struggle with the assumed infallibility of old Hebraic Testament literal instructions, assertions and narratives.

The Old Testament may indeed be, to some extent, the link which binds together thousands of Christians, for Jesus the Christ founded His doctrine upon a Jewish people, but the interminable list of Christian sects of to-day have almost all taken their rise from the assertion of a right of personal interpretation of the Bible, which might have remained debarred to the generality by the confession that the keys of interpretation were lost, or at least missing, and that without their assistance error of a vital character was inevitable.

The vast accumulation of varying interpretations of the Bible, although a folly, yet sinks into insignificance as an incident of importance, before the collateral truth that the followers of each of the hundreds of sects have arrogated to themselves, not only the right of personal interpretation, but the duty of condemning all others--as if the infallibility they claimed for the Bible could not fail to be reflected upon their personal propaganda, or the specialities of a chapel service. Religious intolerance has cursed every village of the land, and hardly a single sect has originated which has not only claimed the right to differ from others, and to criticise, but also to persecute and assign to perdition all beyond its own narrow circle.

The Mystic, the Occultist and the Theosophist do indeed do good, or God, service, by illustrating the bases and origins of all faiths by the mutual illumination that is available. By tolerance and mutual esteem much good may arise, but by the internecine struggles of religionists, every faith is injured, and religion becomes a by-word meaning intolerance, strife and vainglory, and the mark and profession of an earnest sectarian is now that he is ever ready to condemn the efforts of others, in direct opposition to the precept of Jesus the Christ, Who said--"Judge not, that ye be not judged."

One sect of the Jews, the Caraites, successors of the Sadducees, throughout history rejected the Kabalah, and it is necessary to say here that the Hebrew Rabbis of this country of the present day do not follow the practical Kabalah, nor accept all the doctrines of the Dogmatic Kabalah. On the other hand, many famous Christian authors have expressed great sympathy with the Doctrinal Kabalah.

St. Jerome, who died in A.D. 420, in his "Letter to Marcella," gives us all the Kabalistic Divine Names allotted to the Ten Sephiroth. Others were Raymond Lully, 1315; Pope Sixtus the Fourth, 1484; Pic de Mirandola, 1494; Johannes Reuchlin, 1522; H. Cornelius Agrippa, 1535; Jerome Cardan, 1576; Gulielmus Postellus, 1581; John Pistorius, 1608; Jacob Behmen, 1624; the notable English Rosicrucian, Robert Fludd, 1637; Henry More, 1687; the famous Jesuit Athanasius Kircher, 1680; and Knorr von Rosenroth, 1689. To these must be added Eliphaz Levi and

Edouard Schure, two modern French writers on the Occult Sciences, and two English authors, Anna Kingsford and Edward Maitland. The notable German philosopher Spinoza, 1677, regarded the doctrines of the Kabalah with great esteem.

2

THE PRACTICAL KABALAH

Let us take the Practical Kabalah before the Dogmatic; it may perhaps have preceded the Theoretical Philosophy because it was at first concerned with an intimate study of the Pentateuch; a research based upon the theory that every sentence, word and letter were given by Divine Inspiration and that no jot or tittle (the Yod the smallest Hebrew letter) must be neglected. The Rabbis counted every word and letter, and as their numbers were represented by their letters, they counted the numeration of all God names and titles, and all proper names, and the numeration of the phrases recording Divine commands.

The Hebrew letters and numbers were :

Aleph	A	1
Beth	B, V	2
Gimel	G, Gh	3
Daleth	D, Dh	4
Heh	H	5
Vau	O, U, V	6
Zayin	Z	7
Cheth	Ch	8
Teth	T	9
Yod	I, Y	10
Kaph	K, Kh	20
Lamed	L	30
Mem	M	40
Nun	N	50
Samekh	S	60
Ayin	Aa, Ngh	70
Pe	P	80
Tzaddi	Tz	90
Qoph	Q	100
Resh	R	200
Shin	Sh	300
Tau	T, Th	400

There were also several final letters, final K, 500; final M, 600; final N, 700; final P, 800; and final Tz, 900. Note that the Divine Name Jah, JH, numbered 15, and so in common usage the number 15 was always represented by 9 and 6, ThV, Teth and Vau.

The Kabalistic Rabbis granted the natural meaning of the words of the "Torah" or Law books of the Old Testament as a guide to a knowledge of proper conduct in life and as a proper reading for the Synagogue and home but they claimed that each verse and narrative, each law and incident, had also a deeper and concealed meaning of a Mystical character to be found by their calculations, conversions, and substitutions, according to their rules of Gematria, Notaricon, and Temura: the first name is of Greek origin, the second from the Latin, but the third was Hebrew and meant permutation, TMURH, from the root MUR,--changed.

The most famous Rabbi of the Seventeenth century named Menasseh ben Israel, compared the Books of Moses to the body of a man, the commentaries called Mishna to the soul, and the Kabalah he called the Spirit of the soul: "ignorant people may study the first, the learned the second, but the wisest direct their contemplation to the third"; he called the Kabalists,--divine theologians possessed of thirteen rules by which they are enabled to penetrate the mysteries with which the Scriptures abound.

Many Kabalists claimed that their doctrines and methods were brought down from Heaven by Angels to primeval man, and they all believed that the First Four Books of the Pentateuch enshrined their peculiar doctrines as well as narrated histories and laid down laws.

The Zohar says :--If these books of the Torah contain only the tales of, and the words of Esau, Hagar, Laban and Balaam, why are they called--The Perfect Law, The Law of Truth, The True Witness of God?--there must be a hidden meaning. "Woe be to the man who says that The Law (Torah) contains only common sayings and tales: if this were true we might even in our time compose a book of doctrine which would be more respected. No, every word has a sublime sense, and is a heavenly mystery. The Law resembles an angel: to come down on earth a spiritual angel must put on a garment to be known or understood here, so the Law must have clothed itself in a garment of words as a body for men to receive; but the wise look within the garments."

At some periods both the ordinary Jew and even Christian Fathers have made a somewhat similar declaration of a literal and a mystical meaning of scripture. The Talmud in book "Sanhedrin" remarks that Manasseh King of Israel asked whether Moses could not relate something of more value than tales of Timnah a concubine, and Rachel with her mandrakes, and he is answered that there is a concealed meaning in these narrations.

The Christian Father Origen (A.D. 253), in his "Homilies," wrote that everybody should regard these stories, the making of the world in six days, and the planting of trees by God,--as figures of speech under which a recondite sense is concealed. Origen granted a Three-fold meaning,-- somatic, psychic, and pneumatic; or the body of scripture, its soul and its spirit.

Nicholas de Lyra who died in 1340 accepted four modes of interpretation; literal, allegoric, moral, and anagogic or mystical.

In this he nearly follows the scheme of the Zohar ii. 99: in which paragraph there is a parable comparing the Sacred Law to a woman in love who reveals herself to her friend and beloved: first by signs, ramaz; then by whispered words, derush; then by converse with her face veiled, hagadah; and at last she reveals her features and tells all her love, this is sod, association in secret, a mystery.

The late Dr. Anna Kingsford and Edward Maitland were notable Kabalists who always insisted on the concealed meanings underlying the ordinary sense of the old Hebrew writings; and the late H.P. Blavatsky used to declare that the truly ancient texts of ancient religions were susceptible of explanations on seven planes of thought.

The Kabalists discovered deep meanings in each Hebrew letter, common and finals, and found secrets in large letters, misplaced letters and in words spelled in unusual manners. At different times they represented God by an Aleph, A; or by a Yod, I; or by a Shin; or by a Point; or by a Point within a circle; or even by a Triangle; and by a Decad of ten yods.

GEMATRIA was a mode of interpretation by which a name or word having a certain numerical value was deemed to have a relation with some other words having the same number; thus certain numbers became representative of several ideas, and were considered to be interpretative one of the other. For example, Messiah spelled, MShICh, numbered 358, and so does the phrase IBA ShILH, Shiloh shall come; and so this passage in Genesis 49 V. 10, was considered to be a prophesy of the Messiah: note that Nachash, NChSh, the Serpent of Moses, is also 358. The letter Shin, Sh, 300, became an emblem of divinity by corresponding with Ruach Elohim, RUCh ALHIM, the Spirit of the Living God.

NOTARICON, or abbreviation, is of two forms; one word is formed from the initial and final letters of one or more words; or the letters of one name are taken as the initials or finals of the words of a sentence. For example, in Deut. 30 V. 12, Moses asks, Who shall go up for us to Heaven? The initial letters of the original words MI IOLH LNV HShMILH, form the word MILH, mylah, which word means circumcision, and the final letters are IHVH, the name Jehovah: hence it was suggested that circumcision was a feature of the way to God in heaven.

Amen, AMN is from the initials of Adonai melekh namen. "The Lord and faithful king"; and the famous Rabbinic word of power used for talismans AGLA is formed of the initials of the words "Ateh gibur leolam Adonai," "The Lord ever powerful," or Tu potens in saeculum Dominine.

TEMURA is a more complex procedure and has led to an immense variety of curious modes of divination: the letters of a word are transposed according to certain rules and with many limitations: or again, the letters of a word are replaced by other letters as arranged by a definite scheme, often shown in a diagram. For example, a common form was to write one half of the alphabet over the other in reverse order, and so the first letter A was replaced by the last T, and B by Shin, and so on. On this plan the word Sheshak of Jeremiah 25 v. 26, is said to mean Babel: this permutation was known as ATBSh, atbash. On this principle we find twenty-one other possible forms named in order Albat, Abgat, Agdat: the complete set was called "The combinations of Tziruph." Other forms were rational, right, averse and irregular, obtained from a square of 22 spaces in each direction, that is of 484 secondary squares, and then putting a letter in each square in order up and down, and then reading across or diagonally, etc. Of this type is the so-called "Kabalah of Nine Chambers" of the Mark Masons.

A further development of the numerical arts was shown by the modes of Contraction and Extension; thus Jehovah, IHVH 26, was extended to IVD-HA-VV-HA, and so 10, 5, 6, 5 or 26 became 20, 6, 12, 6 or 44. By extension Zain, Z.7, became 1, 2, 3, 4, 5, 6 and 7 or 28; or 28 was regarded as 2 and 8 or 10. The Tetragrammaton, Jehovah 26 was also at times regarded as 2 and 6 or 8: so El Shaddai, God Almighty, AL ShDI, 1, 30, 300, 4, 10, was 345 and then 12 and then 3, a Trinity. A quaint conceit was that of the change of the spelling of the names of Abraham and Sara: at first Abram ABRM and Sarai ShRI, became ABRHM and ShRH: they were 100 and 90 years old and were sterile: now H, Heh, was deemed of a fertile type, and so the letter H was added to ABRAM, and the Yod I, converted into an H of the name Sarai.

In the very old "Sepher Yetzirah" is found the allocation of letters to the planets; from this origin arose a system of designing talismans written on parchment or engraved on brass or gems: as each planet had a letter and a number, in regard to each was allotted a Magic Square of lesser squares; thus for Jupiter 4 was the number and Daleth the letter, and the Magic Square of Jupiter had 16 smaller squares within it; in each a number 1 to 16, and so each line added up to 34 and the total of numbers was 136. Every Talisman duly formed bore at least one God name to sanctify it: notable names were IH, Jah; ALH, Eloah; then IHVH; then the notable 42 lettered Name, which was really composed of others,--Aheie asher aheie (I am that I am) Jah, Jehuiah, Al, Elohim, Jehovah, Tzabaoth, Al Chai and Adonai.

The Shemhamphorash, or Separated Name, was a famous Word of Power; it was formed of Three times 72 letters: the words of three verses, 19, 20 and 21 of Exodus XIV. were taken: the separated letters of verse 19 were written down, then the letters of verse 20 in reverse order, then those of verse 21 in direct order: this gave 72 Names read from above down, each of 3 letters: to each was added either AL or IH, and so were formed the names of the 72 Angels of the Ladder of Jacob which led from earth to heaven: these names were often placed on the obverse and reverse of medals or rolls of parchment to form 36 Talismans.

According to some Kabalists both King David and King Solomon were able to work wonders with Kabalistic Magical Arts: The Pentagram was called the Seal of Solomon, and the Hexagram was called the Shield of David; to the points of the former were assigned the Spirit and Four Elements, while to those of the latter were ascribed the Planets. The treatise called "The Clavicules of King Solomon" is of course a mediaeval fraud.

The Hebrew letters are also associated with the Twenty-two Trumps of the Tarot pack of cards; these cards have been much used for purposes of divination. The Gipsies of Southern Europe use these cards for Fortune-telling. The French author Court de Gebelin (1773-1782) declared that these Trump cards as mystical emblems were derived from the magic of Ancient Egypt. Occult Science allots each card to a Number, a Letter and a natural object or force,-the Planets, Zodiacal signs, elements, etc. "The Sanctum Regnum of the Tarot Trumps" edited by myself can be consulted. Dr. Encausse of Paris, who writes under the pseudonym of "Papus," has also a work relating to the Tarots and gives a Kabalistic attribution of the Trump cards which Rosicrucians consider to be erroneous.

So far as is known to me the practice of Kabalah as a Magical Art is now almost restricted to Russian and Polish Rabbis, and to a few students of occultism in this country, some of whom constantly wear a Kabalistic talisman although they are Christians.

THE DOGMATIC KABALAH

"The great doctrines of the Theoretical Kabalah," says Ginsburg, "are mainly designed to solve the problems of (a) the nature of the Supreme Being, (b) the creation of the Universe and of our world, (c) the creation of angels and man, (d) the destiny of the world and of men, and (e) the import of the revealed law."

The Kabalah confirms the following Old Testament declarations: the Unity of God, His incorporeal form (Deut. chap. iv., v. 15.); eternity, immutability, perfection and goodness; the origin of the world at God's will, the government of the Universe, and the creation of man after the image of God. It seeks to explain by Emanations the transition from the Infinite to the finite, the multitude of forms from a unity; the production of matter from spiritual intelligence; and the relations existing between Creator and creature. In this theosophy,--ex nihil nihilo fit; spirit and matter are the opposite poles of one existence: and as nothing comes from nothing, so nothing is annihilated.

The following seven Kabalistic ideals are of the greatest interest to students of the origin and destiny of the world and mankind.

(1)   That God, the Holy One, the Supreme Incomprehensible One, the AIN SUPh, the Greek apeiros, (Zohar iii. 283) was not the direct Creator of the World; but that all things have proceeded from the Primordial Source in successive Emanations, each one less excellent than the preceding, so that the universe is 'God Manifested,' and the last and remotest production is matter, a privation of perfection.

(2)   That all we perceive or know of, is formed on the Sephirotic type.

(3)   That human souls were pre-existent in an upper world before the origin of this present world.

(4)   That human souls before incarnation dwell now in an Upper Hall, or Treasury where the decision is made as to what earth body each soul or ego shall enter.

(5)   That every soul after earth life or lives must at length be so purified as to be reabsorbed into the Infinite God.

(6)   That one human life is seldom sufficient; that two earth lives are necessary for almost all to pass; and that if failure result in the second life, a third life is passed linked with a stronger soul who draws the sinner upward into purity: this is a form of the scheme of Re-incarnation, Transmigration of souls, or Metempsychosis.

(7)   That when all the pre-existent Souls who have been incarnated here have arrived at perfection, the Evil Angels are also to be raised, and all lives will be merged into The Deity by the Kiss of Love from the Mouth of the Holy One, and the Manifested Universe shall be no more, until again vivified by the Divine FIAT.

It has been suggested by some learned authors that these Kabalistic ideas resemble those of the Alexandrian philosophy and of the Gnostics, embodying notions derived from the Pythagoreans, the Platonists and from Indian Brahmanism and Buddhism.

Let us more fully consider the conceptions of the Divinity. Isaac Myer writes :--God may be regarded from four points of view; as the Eternal One, or AIN SUP, Ain Suph; as AHIH, Aheie, I am; as IHVH, Who was, is and will be; and as ALHIM, Elohim, God in Nature, called Adonai or Lord.

In the English Old Testament the word IHVH is translated Lord, and Elohim by God: Boutell calls Jah a contraction of Jehovah.

The Jehovah of the Old Testament,--as a tribal Deity of personal characteristics, demonstrating His power and glory to a chosen people; oppressing other nations to do them service, and choosing as His special envoys and representatives men whom our civilisation would have condemned as not high enough for Spiritual power, is not represented in the Hebrew Secret Doctrine.

The Kabalah, indeed, is full of Jehovah, IHVH, the Divine Four-Lettered Name, the Tetragrammaton, but it is as the Name of a group of Divine Conceptions, of Emanations from a central Spiritual Light whose presence alone is postulated;

from Absolute God there is a series of Emanations extending downward to reach Jehovah, Who is the Divine One of Binah, the Supernal Mother; other stages of Emanation lead to The Elohim, the group of Holy Spiritual attributes, associated with the Sixth Sephira, the Sun of Tiphareth.

After another manner, Jehovah is the group of the Emanations from the Deific source, called the Ten Sephiroth, "The Voices from Heaven." These Ten Sephiroth, of which the First is a condensation of the Supernal Glory from the Ain Suph Aour, the Boundless Light, appear as a Rainbow of the Divinity in a First World, or highest plane above human conception, that of Atziluth; by successive reflections, diminishing in brightness, a plane is reached which is conceivable by man, as of the purity of his highest spiritual vision. The grouping of the Ten Divine Qualities, upon this plane, into a Divine Tetrad, is symbolised by Yod Heh Vau Heh, the Tetragrammaton, the Kabalistic Jehovah, not the Yahveh of the exoteric books, but the original of that God, whose reflections of a nation's patron is formulated in the Old Testament: it is "The Ineffable Name," never pronounced, its true sound is lost, and the Jew replaces it by Adonai, ADNI; it is unpronounceable because its real vowels are unknown; it ceased to be spoken before the vowel points were introduced. (Note;--there are no extant Hebrew works with vowel points earlier than the tenth century.--A. E. WAITE.)

We find that the Kabalah contemplates a period when Chaos existed, a period of repose and absence of manifestation, when the Negative reigned supreme: this is the Pralaya of the Hindoos. From passivity there proceeded action by Emanations, and Manifested Deity arose. From Ain, repose, the Negative, proceeded Ain Suph, the No-Bound, the Limitless, the Omnipresence of the Unknowable; still condensing into manifestation through Emanation, there appears the Ain Suph Aur, "The Boundless Light," which coalescing on a point appears as Kether, the Crown of Manifestation. Thence follow the Sephiroth, the Holy Voices, upon the Highest World; they concentrate into a divine conception, a stage of Spiritual existence which man attempts to grasp, and by defining, to limit, bound and describe, and so creates for his worship a Divine personality, his God; and the Jew named Him, --Jehovah.

By gradual stages of development, each farther from the source, there arise the powers and forces which have received the names of Archangels,

Angels, Planetary Spirits, and the guardians of man; still farther from God, we obtain the human Souls, which are as Sparks of Light, struck off from the insupportable Light of Divinity, which have been formulated into Egoity to pass through a long series of changes and experiences by which they make the circuit of a Universe; they endure every stage of existence, of separation from the Divine fountain, to be at last once more indrawn to the Godhead, The Father, whence they emerged upon a pilgrimage; they follow a regular succession of evolution and involution, even as the Divine passes ever along in successive periods of outbreathing and inbreathing, of Manifestation and of Repose.

Of Divine Repose, or Chaos, the human intellect can form no conception, and only the highly spiritual man can conceive any of the sublime and exalted stages of Manifestation. To the worldly man such notions are but dreams, and any attempt to formulate them leads only to suspicions of one's sanity. To the metaphysician these ideals supply a theme of intense interest; to the theosophist they supply an illustration drawn from a foreign source of the Spiritual traditions of a long-past age, which lead one to accept the suggestion that these Spiritual conceptions are supplied from time to time by a Great Mind of another stage of existence from our own. Perhaps they are remnants of the faiths and wisdom of a long-vanished era, which had seen the life-history of races more spiritual than our own and more open to converse with the Holy Ones of higher Spiritual planes. Spiritual wisdom can only be attained by the man, or earthly being who becomes able to reach up to the sphere above; a Spiritual Being above us cannot reach down and help those who do not so purify themselves that they may be fit to rise up to the higher planes of existence.

The chief difficulty of the beginner as a student of the Kabalah, is to conquer the impressions of the reality and materiality of so-called matter. The Kabalah teaches that one must entirely relinquish the apparent knowledge of matter as an entity apart from Spirit. The assertion that matter exists, and is an entity entirely different from Spirit, and that Spirit--the God of Spirits--created it, must be denied, and the notion must be torn out by the roots before progress can be made. If matter exists, it is something, and must have come from some-thing; but Spirit is not a thing, and creative Spirit, the highest Spiritual conception, could not make matter, the lowest thing, out of nothing: hence it is not made, and hence there is no matter. All is Spirit and conception. Ex nihilo nihil fit. All that does exist can only have come from Spirit, from Divine Essence. That Being should arise from non-being is impossible. That matter should create itself is absurd; matter cannot proceed from Spirit; the two words mean that the two ideas are entirely apart; then matter cannot exist. Hence it follows that what we call matter is but an aspect, a conception, an illusion, a mode of motion, a delusion of our physical senses.

Apart from the Kabalah, the same truth has been recognised by a few exceptional Christians and Philosophers. What is commonly known as the "Ideal Theory" was promulgated 140 years ago by Berkeley, Bishop of Cloyne in Ireland; it is nearly identical with the Kabalistic doctrine of all things being but Emanations from a Divine source, and matter but an aspect. Other philosophers have discussed the same theory in the controversy of Nominalism versus Realism: does anything exist except in name? Is there any substratum below the name of anything? Need we postulate any such basis? All is Spirit,--says the Kabalah,--and this is eternal, uncreated; intellectual and sentient on our plane; inhering are life and motion; It is self-existing, with succesive waves of action and passivity. This Spirit is the true Deity, or Infinite Being, the "Ain Suph," the Cause of all causes, and of all effects. All emanates from "That," and is in "That." The Universe is an immanent offspring of the Divine, which is manifested in a million forms of differentiation. The Universe is yet distinct from God, even as an effect is distinct from a cause; yet it is not apart from Deity, it is not a transient effect, it is immanent in the Cause. It is God made manifest to Man. Matter is our conception alone; it represents the aspect of the lowest manifestation of Spirit, or Spirit is the highest manifestation of matter. Spirit is the only substance. "Matter," says a Kabalist, "is the mere residuum of emanation, but little above non-entity." The Hindoo philosopher called matter a Maya, a delusion.

As already remarked the Supreme Being of the Kabalah is found to be demonstrated in more than one aspect. At one time the Inconceivable Eternal Power proceeding by successive Emanations into a more and more humanly conceivable existence, formulating His attributes into conceptions of Wisdom, Beauty, Power, Mercy and Governance;

exhibiting these attributes first in a supernal universality beyond the ken of all spirits, angels and men, the First Word of Atziluth; then formulating a reflection of the same exalted essences on the plane of the Pure Spirits also inconceivable to man, the Second Word of Briah. Again is the reflection repeated, and the Divine Essence in its group of exalted attributes is cognisable to the Angelic Powers, the Third or Yetziratic World; and then finally the Divine abstractions of the Sacred Ten Sephiroth are by a last Emanation still more restricted and condensed than the latter, and are rendered conceivable by the Human intellect; for man exists in the Fourth World of Assiah in the shadow of the Tenth Sephira--the Malkuth, or Kingdom of the World of Shells or material objects. Small wonder then at the slightness of the ideal man can form of the Divine.

At other times we find the metaphysical abstract laid aside, and all the wealth of Oriental imagery lavished on the description of God; imagery although grouped and clustered around the emblem of an exalted humanity, yet so inflated, so extravagantly magnified, that the Heavenly man is lost sight of in the grandeur and tenuity of the word painting of the Divine portrait. Divine anthropomorphism it may be, but an anthropomorphism so tenuous by means of its grandeur, that the human elements affording the bases of the analogy quite disappear in the Heavenly Man of their divine reveries.

Permit me to afford to you an example of one sublime, deific dream:--

"In this conformation He is known; He is the Eternal of the Eternal ones; the Ancient of the Ancient ones; the Concealed of the Concealed ones; in His symbols He is knowable although He is unknowable. White are His garments, and His appearance is as a Face, vast and terrible in its vastness. Upon a throne of flaming brilliance is He seated, so that he may direct its flashing Rays. Into many thousand worlds the brightness of His face is extended, and from the Light of this brightness the just shall receive worlds of joy and reward in the existence to come. Within His skull exist daily a thousand myriads of worlds; all draw their existence from Him, and by Him are upheld. From that Head distilleth a Dew, and from that Dew which floweth down upon the worlds, are the dead raised up in the lives and on the worlds to come."

The God of the Kabalah is "Infinite Existence": He cannot be defined as the "Assemblage of Lives," nor is he truly the "totality of his attributes." Yet without deeming all lives to be of Him, and His attributes to be universal, He cannot be known by man. He existed before He caused the Emanations of H is essence to be demonstrated, He was before all that exists is, before all lives on our plane, or the plane above, or the World of pure Spirits, or the Inconceivable existence; but then He resembled nothing we can conceive, and was Ain Suph, and in the highest abstraction Ain, alone, Negative Existence. Yet before the manifest became demonstrated, all existence was in him; the Known preexisted in the Unknown, Who is the "Ancient of Days."

But it is not this dream-like aspect of poetic phantasy exhibited in the Kabalah that I can further bring to your notice. Let us return to the Philosophic view of the attributes of Deity, which is the keynote of the whole of the doctrine.

The primary human conception of God is then the Passive state of Negative Existence AIN--not active; from this the mind of man passes to conceive of AIN SUPh, of God as the Boundless, the Unlimited, Undifferentiated, Illimitable

One; and the third stage is AIN SUPh AUR--Boundless Light, Universal Light--"Let there be Light" was formulated, and "There was Light." The Passive has put on Activity; the Conscious God has awaked. Let us now endeavour to conceive of the concentration of this effulgence, let us formulate a gathering together of the rays of this illumination into a Crown of glorified radiance, and we recognise KTR, Kether, the Crown, the First Sephira, First Emanation of Incomprehensible Deity, the first conceivable attribute of immanent manifested Godhead: also named ADM OILAH, Adam Oilah, The Heavenly Man, and Autik Yomin, The Ancient of days. The devout Rabbi bows his head and adores the sublime conception. He is represented in the Hebrew Old Testament by the Divine Name AHIH, Aheieh, "I am " (Exodus iii. v. 4).

The conscious God having arisen in His energy, there follow immediately two further Emanations, the Trio shining in the symbol of a radiant triangle. ChKMH, Chokmah, Wisdom, The King, with the Divine Name IH, Jah is the Second Sephira; BINH, Binah, Understanding, The Queen, and the Divine Name IHVH Jehovah is the Third Sephira,--the Supernal Triad" is demonstrated.

Then follow GDULH, Gedulah, also called CHSD, Chesed, Mercy, with the Divine Name AL, El; and its contrast GBURH, Geburah, Severity, also called Pachad, Fear, with the Divine Name ALH, Eloah; and the reflected triangle is completed by the Sixth Sephira, the Sun, named TPART, Tiphareth, or Beauty, with the name ALHIM Elohim; considered as a triangle of reflection with the apex below. The third triangle may be considered as a second reflection with the apex below; it is formed of the seventh, eighth, and ninth Sephiroth; NTzCh, Netzach, Firmness or Victory, with the name Jehovah Sabaoth; HUD, Hod or Hud, Splendour, with the name Elohim Sabaoth; and ISUD, Yesod, Foundation, with the name AL ChAI, El Chai.

Finally, all these ideals are resumed in a single form, the Tenth Sephira, MLKUT, Malkuth, the Shekinah, the Kingdom, also sometimes called Tzedek, Righteousness. The whole Decad form "Adam Kadmon," "The Archetypal Man," and the wondrous OTz ChIIM, "Tree of Life." In the ancient figures of Adam Kadmon we see Kether, the Crown, over the forehead; Chokmah and Binah are the two halves of the thinking brain; Gedulah and Geburah are the organs of action, the right and left upper limbs; Tiphareth

is the heart and the vital organs of the chest; Netzach and Hud are the lower limbs right and left; Jesod refers to the digestive and reproductive organs and abdomen; and lastly Malkuth is compared to the feet as a basis or foundation of man upon this earth or lowest plane: see the plate of The Adam Kadmon, Archetypal Man, or The First Adam.

These Triads were looked upon as formed of a Principle of Union and a male and female potency, and thus a Balance, MTQLA, Methequela, exists.

Almost as old as the Kabalistic doctrine of the Sephiroth, the Intelligences, or Emanations, are the peculiar forms in which they were represented in diagrams which resume all Kabalistic ideas, and are emblems of these views on every subject. Every Deific conception can be thus demonstrated, and also the constitution of the Angelic Hosts, the principles of Man's Nature, the group of Planetary Bodies, the Metallic elements, the Zigzag flash of the Lightning and the composition of the sacred Tetragrammaton, the Mystical Jehovah, IHVH, Yod, Heh, Vau, Heh, numbering 26. See Plates I., II., III., IV., V., and VI. This Decad of Deific Emanations is to be conceived as first formulated on the Divine First plane of Atziluth, which is entirely beyond our ken; to be reproduced on the Second plane of pure Spirit, Briah; to exist in the same Decad form in the world of Yetzirah, the Third or Formative plane; and finally to be sufficiently condensed as to be cognizable by the human intellect on the Fourth plane of Assiah, on which we seem to exist. From our point of view we may regard the "Tree of Life" as a type of many divine processes and forms of manifestation, but these are symbols we use to classify our ideals, and we must not debase the divine Emanations by asserting these views of the Sephiroth are real, but only as conceivable by humanity.

For example, the Kabalah demonstrates the grouping of the Ten Sephiroth into Three Pillars; the Pillar of Mercy, the Pillar of Severity, and the Pillar of Mildness between them: these may also be associated with the Three Mother Letters, A, M, Sh; Aleph, Mem and Shin. Then again by two horizontal lines we may form three groups and consider these Sephiroth to become types of the

Three divisions of Man's Nature, the Intellectual, Moral, and Sensuous (neglecting Malkuth, the material body), thus connecting the Kabalah with Mental and Moral Philosophy and Ethics. By three lines again we consider the Sephiroth to be divisible into Four Planes., upon each of which I have already said you must conceive the whole Ten Sephiroth to be immanent. By a series of Six lines we group them into Seven planes referable to the worlds of the Seven Planetary powers, thus connecting the Kabalah with Astrology. (W. Gorn Old has recently published a volume called "Kabalistic Astrology.")

To each Sephira were allotted in Briah an especial Archangel, and in Yetzirah an army of Angels; these connect the Kabalah with Talismanic Magic. There is also a close relation between the old Kabalistic theology and Alchymy; each Sephira of Assiah becomes the allegoric emblem of one of the metals: and there is a special Rabbinic volume named "Asch Metzareph" entirely concerned with Alchymy; its name in English meaning is "Cleansing Fires." (My English translation can be obtained.) A. E. Waite in his work on the Kabalah states that Rabbi Azariel ben Menachem in his "Commentary on the Sephiroth" allots a particular colour to each one, but these do not agree with the colours given in the Zohar, where we find Kether called colourless, Tiphareth purple, and Malkuth sapphire-blue.

These Ten Sephiroth are thought of as being connected together by "Paths," Twenty-two in number, shown on the Diagram; they are numbered by means of the letters of the Hebrew Alphabet, each of which being equally a letter and a number. The 22 Trumps of the pack of Tarot cards (Tarocchi) are also related to these Paths. The 22 Paths, added to the 10 Sephiroth form the famous "Thirty-two Ways" by which Wisdom descends by successive stages upon Man, and may enable him to mount to the Source of Wisdom by passing successively upward through these 32 Paths. This process of mental Abstraction was the Rabbinic form of what the Hindoo knows as Yoga, or the Union of the human with the Divine, by contemplation and absorption of the mind in a mystical reverie.

Frequently quoted Kabalistic words are: Arikh Anpin, Makroprosopos, the Vast Countenance which is a title of Kether the Crown, Deity Supreme; Zauir Anpin, Mikroprosopos, the Lesser Countenance is the Central Sun,

Tiphereth, a conception that has something in common with that of the Christian Christ, the Son of God. (The former was represented by a face in profile, the latter by the full face. M. Mathers). Binah is the Supernal Mother, Aima. Malkuth is the Inferior Mother, the Bride of the Mikroprosopos. Daath or Knowledge is the union of Chokmah and Binah, of wisdom and understanding. Merkabah was the Chariot Throne of God of the vision of Ezekiel mentioned in his chapters i. and x.; it rested on wheels and was carried by Four Cherubim, the Sacred Animal Forms, which resembled the Man, Lion, Bull and Eagle, which were related to the Four quarters of the World, and to Four types of humanity.

The Four Letters Yod, He, Vau, He, or as we say IHVH, of the name we call Jehovah, are allotted and distributed by the Kabalistic doctrine among the Sephiroth in a peculiar manner, forming the mysterious conception of the Tetragrammaton, that awful name of Divine Majesty which might never be uttered by the common people, and whose true pronunciation has been for many centuries confessedly lost to the Jews and has never been known to the Christians.

The views of the Kabalists on Cosmogony are not easy to explain, but as before said the Supreme Boundless God, the "Ain Suph" was not the direct Creator of the World, nor was the world made out of nothing.

The highest Trinity of "The Crown, King and Queen" having arisen by Divine Emanation, its powers descended and expanded into the Seven Lower Sephiroth, and produced the Universe in their own image, a decad of forces, as a whole constituting the ADM QDMUN Adam Quadmun, or Adam Kadmon, the Primordial or Archetypal Man; the world produced is the existing Universe of which we have cognizance. The universe is called the "Garment of God": this lower world is a copy of the Divine World, everything here has its prototype above. (Zohar ii. 20.)

Some Kabalistic treatises speak of earlier worlds created before the conjunction of the Divine King and Queen; these perished in the void; these lost worlds are referred to in Genesis 36, v. 31-40, as "The Kings of Edom who reigned before Israel," they are said to have perished one after the other; these worlds were convulsed and were no more known.

Having considered the Divine Emanations, and the origin of the Universe, I must refer to the spiritual beings of the Four Worlds. In the First purest and highest World of Atziluth there dwell only the Primary Ten Sephiroth of the Adam Oilah or Archetype, perfect and immutable.

In the Second World of Briah reside the Archangels headed by "Metatron" related to Kether, in solemn grandeur; He is the garment of Al Shaddai, the visible manifestation of God; the Number of both is 314 (Zohar iii. 231a). The word Metatron meant "The Great Teacher." It has a curious resemblance to the Greek words met thronon, beside or beneath the throne of God; but this derivation is fanciful. He rules the other Archangels of the Universe, who govern in their courses all the heavenly bodies, and the evolutions of the dwellers on them: He is, according to the Kabalists, the efficient God of our Earth,--the Greek Demiourgos. The other Arch-Angels are according to Macgregor Mathers, Ratziel, Tzaphkiel, Tzadquiel, Kamael, Michael, Haniel, Raphael, Gabriel, and Sandalphon.

In the Third World of Yetzirah are the Ten hosts of Angelic beings, a separate class for each Sephira; they are intelligent incorporeal beings, clothed in a garment of light, and are set over the several heavenly bodies, the planets, over the elemental forces, and over seasons, times, etc.; they are the officers of the great Arch-Angels. The Hosts of Angels of the Sephiroth are Chaioth ha kodesh, Auphanim, Arelim, Chashmalim, Seraphim, Melakim, Elohim, Beni Elohim, Cherubim, and tenthly the Ishim who are the Beatified Souls of men and women.

The Fourth World of Assiah is filled with the lowest beings, the Evil Demons, Kliphoth or Qliphoth, the cortices or shells, and with all so-called material objects, and to this world belong men, the Egos or Souls imprisoned in earthly human bodies. This world also has its ten grades, each one more far from the higher forces and forms, each one more dark and impure. First come THU, Tohu, the Formless; and BHU, Bohu, the Void, thirdly ChShK, the Darkness, of the early universe, and from these our world was developed and now exists; then come seven hells, whose dwellers are evil beings representing all human sins; their rulers are Samael or Satan the angel of death, and Lilith, the Asheth Zenunim, the Woman of whoredom, and this pair of demons are also called "The Beast," see Zohar ii. 255; Samael had also an incommunicable name, which was IHVH reversed; for Demon est Deus inversus.

The whole universe only became complete with the creation of Man, called the Microcosm, the Earthly Adam; a copy of "The Archetypal Man" after another manner; he has principles and faculties and forms comparable to all the Sephiroth and Worlds, although his material body dwells on the Assiatic plane.

From God, the Angels and the World, let us pass to consider more fully what the Kabalah teaches about Man, the human Soul or Ego.

It has already been explained that the Doctrine of Emanation postulates successive stages of the manifestation of the Supreme Spirit, which may be regarded as existing on separate planes. Now the Ten Sephiroth condense their energy into a formulated Four-parted group of Three Spiritual planes, and a plane of so-called Objectivity, or of Matter. These Ten Sephiroth, and the planes, each contribute an essence which in their totality, in ever-varying proportion, constitutes Man. At his origin there was formulated what the scientists might call "Archetypal Man," and what the Kabalists named Adam Kadmon, ADM QDMUN.

Primeval Man, the Greek protogonos. Successive stages of beings of this type pass along the ages through a descending scale, offering the individual every variety of experience, and then along an ascending scale of redevelopment until human perfection is attained, and ultimate reunion with the Divine is the result of the purified Soul having completed its pilgrimage.

Before we consider Man in his present state we must note the views of the Kabalah upon Man in his primal state.

Man was the final Word of Creation, he was a resume of all forms, and so transcended the angels in his faculties. The first man had no fleshy body, no material envelope: Adam and Eve were clothed only in ethereal forms, and were not subject to appetites or passions, they dwelled in Light in the GN OiDN, Garden of Aidin, of Eden, of pleasant peace (Zohar ii. 229b). The man and the woman before their descent to this world were as one,-- androgynous; at incarnation they were separated into sexes. The first human pair broke the first commandment, they sinned and were doomed to a complete descent into matter; the Lord God made them "coats of skin," He gave them material bodies, and with these came the need of food, and the passions required to bring forth a succession of earthly bodies.

Yet man is still the copy of God on earth; his form is related to the Tetragrammaton of Jehovah IHVH, for in a diagram, Yod is as the head, Heh the arms, Vau the body, and the final Heh the lower limbs: (see Zohar ii. 42a). The first pair were tempted by Samael, the allegorical Personality of the lower tendencies, which give the craving to experience earth life and take a part in its continuous changes of force and form. They did what they knew would imperil their purely psychic existence, they sank fully into material forms, they took on the grossness of Malkuth, and so were separated from the Sephirotic Tree, from the Higher Potencies, which have no taint of matter. All matter is ever changing its form, and so their bodies must be changed; their bodies died, and so must the bodies of all incarnated Egos; at death the personality passes away to a rest, and then to a further experience of life, or to a sphere of punishment, or to a realm of bliss.

In their earthly forms they brought forth bodies like their own, and God sent down other souls to dwell in them, to experience earth life, its sins and sufferings; and to pass a probation by which they also might fall, but yet may rise to regain a share of man's lost estate and finally to rise up through the Sephiroth to a reunion with the Divine Essence.

Remember that the Sephirotic Crown was First, then came Chokmah, a masculine Potency, and then Binah, a feminine one; from their union arose the created universe of angels, men and earth: but 'as above so below,' so we have in Genesis a Man formed, then succeeds a Woman, and from them all others.

In the " Commentary on the Creation of Genesis," still allegorical like Genesis itself, it is stated :--
"There is in Heaven a treasury called GUP, Guph, and all the Souls which were created in the beginning, and hereafter to come into this world, The Holy One placed therein: out of this treasury The Holy One furnishes children in the womb with Souls."

A further commentary in symbolic language narrates how The Holy One perceiving a child's body to be in formation, sends for a suitable Ego to inhabit it.

"The Holy One, blessed be He, beckons to an Angel who is set over the disembodied souls, and says to him, 'Bring me such a soul': and this is being always done since the world began; the soul appears before the Holy One and worships in His presence, to whom the Eternal One says :--'Betake thyself to this form.' Instantly the soul excuses himself, saying, 'Oh Governor of the World, I am satisfied with the world in which I have been so long: if it please Thee, do not force me into this foul body, for I am a Spirit.' The Holy One, blessed be He, answers: 'The world I am about to send thee into is needed for thee, it is to pass down through it that I formed thee from myself.' And so the soul is forced to incarnate and sink into the world where matter will imprison him, where he must suffer, but where he may overcome and from whence he must rise again. The Zohar adds the statement: "and whatever the man learns and displays on earth life, he knew before his incarnation."

This is a parallel doctrine to the Buddhist scheme of Re-incarnation with Karma as God-eternal law, relentlessly compelling the individual Ego to a new earth life.

Christian Ginsburg states that a "Transmigration of Souls" was the belief of the Pharisees in the time of Josephus; and this dogma was held by many Jews up to the ninth century of our era. The

Caraite Jews have accepted it ever since the seventh century. St. Jerome says it was a doctrine of the early Christian Church taught only to a select few believers, and Origen was of opinion that without transmigration, the incidents of the struggle between Esau and Jacob before birth, Genesis 25, v. 22, and the reference to Jeremiah in the mother's womb could not be explained, Jer. i. 5.

The Kabalah then teaches that the Egos have come out from the Spirit Fountain, suffer incarnation again and again until experience and perfection have been attained, and ultimately rejoin the Divine Source: Zohar i. 145, 168; ii. 97.

Now what is it that dwells for a time in this 'Coat of Skin," as Genesis in chapter 3, v. 21, calls it, this so-called material body? It is a Divine Spark, composed of several elements derived from the symbolic Four Parts of Jehovah, and from Three Worlds, and these are seated in the Fourth World of Effects, the Material Universe. Now it is no doubt true that in the several Kabalistic schools, the numbers and names of these Essences vary, but the basal idea remains the same: just in a similar way the principles of Man's constitution, as stated in different Hindoo books, also vary, but the root idea is the same in them all.

The Human Principles may be stated as Three in a fourth--the body; or as Five, recognising Astral form and material body; or as Seven, subdividing the divine principle; or as Ten, comparable to the Sephiroth. To explain these fully would take a long essay and would require many Hebrew abstruse words, a difficulty to those who are unused to them: two systems will suffice as an illustration.

From Yod, the Je of Jehovah, comes the highest over-shadowing of the Divine, comparable to the Atma of the Indian philosophies. From He, the ho of Jehovah, comes Neshamah, the Buddhi of the Hindoos, the spiritual soul. From Vau, the v of Jehovah, comes Ruach, the Manas of the Hindoos, Intellect and Mind. From the final He, the ah of Jehovah, is derived Nephesh, the Kama of the Hindoos, the appetites and passions.

These are all implanted in the Astral shell, which moulds the physical body, the instrument which acts upon material objects.

The Human Soul is again conceived of as distributed through several distinct forms of conscious manifestation related to the "Ten

Sephiroth": the several Kabalistic treatises give several groupings, which are all relevant one to the other, the most usual one being a triple division, into Nephesh, the passions referred to Malkuth; Ruach, the Mind, Reason, and Intellect referred to the group of Six Sephiroth lying around the Sun of Tiphereth; and Neshamah, the spiritual aspirations associated with the Supernal Triangle of the Queen, King and Crown.

These Human principles function upon Four Worlds,--Divine, Moral, Intellectual and Emotional respectively: and either of these essences may dominate a man, and they do, in fact, exist in constantly varying proportions. The highest principle overshadows the others, and the central ones may reach up to the higher; or by neglect of opportunities, or by vicious actions, may fall lower and lower, so as to approximate to the seeming matter of the body. As the Neshamah draws one to Spiritual excellence, so the Nephesh leads down to physical enjoyment.

In another form of symbolism the Kabalist tells us a man has two companions, or guides; one on the right, Yetzer ha Tob, to good acts, he is from the higher Sephiroth; and one on the left, Yetzer ha Ra, encouraging the appetites and passions, temptations to evil, is an agent of Samael and of The Beast. Man is in a very unfortunate position according to the Zohar 95 b, for it is there said that the Evil Angel joins him at birth, but the Good Angel only at the age of 13 years.

As to Death, as we have already learned, the man's Ego or Soul, unless the life has been super-excellent, has to be re-born in another form, but at death, as all religions agree, great changes occur. According to the Kabalah, the visible material body, the Guph, decays, and the Animal aspect of the soul, the Nephesh, only gradually fades away from it: the Ruach, the Human aspect, passes away from the Assiatic plane, and the Neshamah, the spiritual soul, returns to the Treasury of Heaven, to the Gan Oidin, or of Paradise, perfected to a Spiritual world beyond the plain of rebirths. The "Sepher jareh chattaim" says that a man is judged in the same hour in which he dies; for the Shekinah, a Presence of the Divine One, comes near him, with three Angels, of whom the chief is Dumah, the Angel of Silence: if the soul is condemned, Dumah takes it to Gai-Hinnom, or hell, for a period of punishment before the next incarnation; if approved, the Soul passes to an Oidin or Heaven. In the end of the present manifestation of the Universe, all souls will have become perfected by suffering, have been blessed in Paradise, and will be in re-union with the God from Whom they came forth.

The Kabalistic theory of man's constitution, origin and destiny is very different from the modern Christian view, but differs from the Indian schemes more in manner of presentation than in principle, and these two may be fitly studied side by side and each will illuminate the other. There is, indeed, no sharp line of cleavage between the Western mystic doctrines, the Kabalism of the Middle Ages related to the Egyptian Hermeticism, and the Indian Esoteric Theosophy. They differ in language nomenclature, and in the imagery employed in the effort to represent spiritual ideas to mankind; but there is no sufficient reason for any condemnation of either school by any other. The world of intellectual culture is wide enough for both to exist side by side, and the mere fact that they are philosophic Systems in any way comprehensible to men is evidence that either can be composed of pure and unveiled truth, for we are still only able to see as in a glass darkly, and must make much further progress before we can hope to see God face to face and know Him as He is.

We must be content to progress, as students have ever done, by stages of development; in each grade the primal truths are re-stated in a different form; they are revealed or reveiled in language and symbolism suitable to the learner's own mental condition; hence the need of a teacher, of a guide who has traversed the path, and who can recognise by personal communion the stage which each pupil has attained. There is no royal or easy path to high attainment in Mysticism. Unwearied effort, combined with purity of life, is of vital importance. The human intellect can only appreciate and assimilate that which the mind's eye can at any time perceive. The process cannot be forced. Mystic lore cannot be stolen. If any learner did appropriate the knowledge of a Grade beyond him it would be to him but folly, disappointment and darkness.

Students have often been offered a doctrine, or assertion, or explanation, which their intellect has rejected as absurd, or as sheer superstition; which same dogma they have later in life assimilated with every feeling of esteem. Occultism in this resembles Freemasonry; we are either admitted to the hidden knowledge, or we are not; and if we are not admitted, we never believe any secret of its ritual even if it be offered to us. The secrets of Occultism are like Freemasonry; in truth they are to some extent the secrets that Freemasonry has lost. They are of their very nature inviolable; for they can only be attained by personal progress; they might be plainly told to the outsider, and not be understood by him. For if anyone has been able to divine and to grasp such a secret, he will not tell it even to his dearest friend; for the simple reason that if his friend is unable to divine it for himself, its communication in mere words would not confer the hidden knowledge upon him.

The whole Kabalistic theories are of a nature similar to the secrets of Freemasonry; there was much doctrine that was never written nor printed: these works often describe imagery which seems folly, and contain doctrines that at first seem absurd; yet they enshrine the highly spiritual teachings which I have shortly outlined. The mere reading of these volumes is of little avail; the spiritual eye needs to be opened to see spiritual things; and the great Kabalists of old did not cast pearls of wisdom before the ignorant or the vicious, nor suffer the unclean to enter the Temple of Wisdom. The serious student must make strenuous efforts to attain to the higher life of the True Occultism, then perchance in a distant future, a record of temptations avoided, and of a life of self-sacrifice may serve as Signs and Pass Words to secure admission to the Palace of the Great King.